OPPORTUNITY

THE JOURNEY FROM YOU TO YES

OPPORTUNITY

THE JOURNEY FROM **YOU TO YES**

ATUL PURI

Worldwide Published by

Pendown Press

PENDOWN PRESS

An ISO 9001 & ISO 14001 Certified Co.,

Regd. Office: 2525/193, 1st Floor, Onkar Nagar-A,
Tri Nagar, Delhi-110035
Ph.: 09350849407, 09312235086
E-mail: info@pendownpress.com
Branch Office: 1A/2A, 20, Hari Sadan, Ansari Road,
Daryaganj, New Delhi-110002
Ph.: 011-45794768
Website: PendownPress.com

First Edition: 2021
Price: ₹259/-
ISBN: 978-93-90479-54-2

Layout and Cover Designed by Pendown Graphics Team
Printed and Bound in India by Thomson Press India Ltd.

AN ODE TO MY MOTHER

This book is exceptional. I completed the draft a few months back, and somehow or the other, I never managed to give the go-ahead to the content such that it could go into print.

The 2nd wave of COVID impacted our life beyond repair:

- Amit, my brother, was infected with COVID and spent 15 days in the hospital.
- My sister lost her father in law, Mr B.P Gupta.
- We lost our mother, Mrs Usha Puri, Founder Director EBN Learning Pvt. Ltd.
- I was hospitalized for 10 days.
- As Amit and I returned from the hospital, we had lost a lot of body mass due to the intake of steroids.
- The next few weeks were very challenging; the body was very weak.

- Headache, body ache, boils, and other unpredictable symptoms kept cropping up.
- Life came to a grinding halt.

I would start panting even if I spoke for a few minutes.

We had so many loose ends to tie up. We were at our wit's end on where to begin. I would cry now and then, thinking of what happened.

This was the ebb of my life. And ironically, the book I was writing is called OPPORTUNITY– The Journey from You to Yes.

Every day I would seek directions to the way forward from mummy. After a complete standstill of 6 weeks, life finally started to turn around:

- I delivered my first Strategy Class – Back To Business – Get > Set > Go on 12th April 2021
- We had an overwhelming response; a few participants even joined from Dubai
- TLM BLUEPRINT happened on 15, 16 and 17th April
- We are starting with UBUNTU (3 months program) as this book goes into print
- I also got an opportunity from M Square Global Education Solutions Inc. to head their Sales and Marketing initiative
- A whole new world of opportunities has opened up.
- As this book goes into print, I must say I have experienced OPPORTUNITY– The Journey from You (me) to Yes in reality. I have lived every word published here during the previous 2 months.

Incidentally, today as I write this section, it is Father's day. I am sure papa is watching me and has been showering his blessings on me.

In gratitude to be born to both of you.

– Atul Puri

CONTENTS

MESSAGE FROM THE AUTHOR

Dear Reader,

'I'm honoured that you have picked up this book. I sincerely hope that this book allows you to have a new perspective on your business.

May this new perspective allow you to infuse a new life into your business that lasts a millennium!

OPPORTUNITY – "The Journey from You to Yes" is a part of The Leverage Model,based on the design thinking approach for an enterprise. I have worked closely with many entrepreneurs, solopreneurs and business owners to create this model.

This book is the outcome of my conversations with entrepreneurs across India. I travelled across the length and breadth of India over three years.

"OPPORTUNITY – The Journey from You to Yes" will enable you to create new realities all around you. It will prove to be a massive contribution to your success in business.

For this purpose, I have kept this book very simple. There is a very clear pattern. In every chapter, we have taken one word, and gone deeper into it to create something meaningful for you, the Reader.

Start the Journey from "You to Yes!"

Warm Regards

Atul Puri
Creator of The Leverage Model and eGrowth Framework

FOREWORD

There are many sources for new venture opportunities for individuals. When you see inefficiency in the market, and you have an idea of how to correct that inefficiency, and you have the resources and capability — or at least the ability to bring together the resources and capability needed to correct that inefficiency, it becomes your responsibility to do so.

OPPORTUNITY - "The Journey from You to Yes" will be extremely helpful to all entrepreneurs. Thank you Mr. Puri for this book which will clear the key question that all would be entrepreneurs face in identifying the business opportunity that is right for them.

Harjinder Singh Cheema
Chairman, Cheema Boilers Limited

LET'S UNDERSTAND THE CONTEXT BEFORE DIVING IN

I value every second of the time that you have chosen to spend with me. What you are about to read has the potential to radically alter the way you conduct your business.

Well-designed structures never fail. This is true for all areas of life and this is equally applicable for businesses. As we look at the genesis of business growth, we observe that the most successful companies have well defined systems and structures. Well-designed structures never fail. This is true for all areas of life and is equally applicable for businesses. As we look at the genesis of business growth, we observe that the most successful companies have well-defined systems and structures.

The Leverage Model

In 2019 I published G.O.L.F. Mastering Business Success in which I shared "The Leverage Model", a framework for highly successful businesses. This is a concentric model having 4 modules – Future, Lifeline, Opportunity and Game Design.

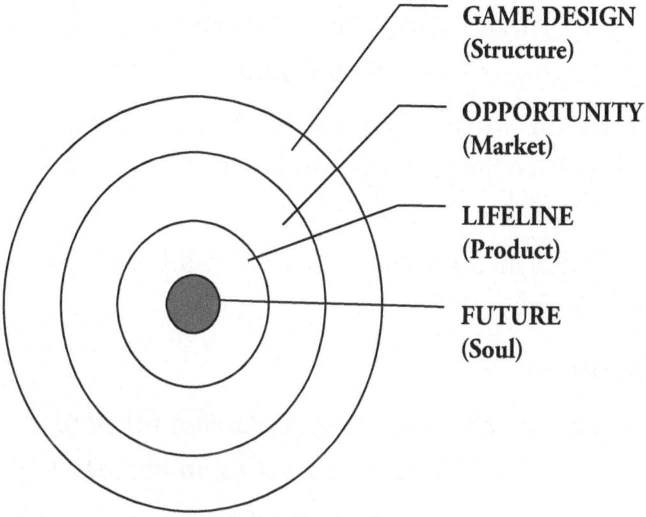

Future

"The journey of a thousand miles
begins with a single "step"

– Lao Tzu

I call this designing the future. Unless you know where you are headed, there are no chances of arriving where you wish to reach. For a business, it is equally valid to zero down on where they are headed.

Lifeline

"Don't find customers for your products,
find products for your customers"
– Seth Godin

The reason for the existence of a business is to serve. This service is delivered either as a product or service. The product/service is the lifeline of the business.

A well designed product or service will bind the customers to your business.

Opportunity

"The entrepreneur always searches for change,
responds to it, and exploits it as an opportunity"
– Peter Drucker

Once you know what you are up to and what you are offering, the next thing to be zeroed on is your market. This is the opportunity your business goes after.

Game Design

"Good design is good business"
– Thomas Watson Jr.

Once you have the three elements in place it's time to tie them together in to a Game Design. The interesting fact of a Game design is that it is done with no constraints. This creates a lot of new possibilities and lays the foundation for a robust business.

In the remaining pages of this book we will explore Opportunity further.

OPPORTUNITY

An opportunity is a set of favourable circumstances that makes it possible to do something. Through this book I am documenting what it takes to create such an environment.

"Your business is a machine to convert the customer's money into your profit"

Digging deeper into this statement, we understand that marketing is an exercise to attract the customer. The outcome of marketing is an opportunity. An opportunity when converted becomes a sale that translates into revenue and profit is an outcome of the revenue.

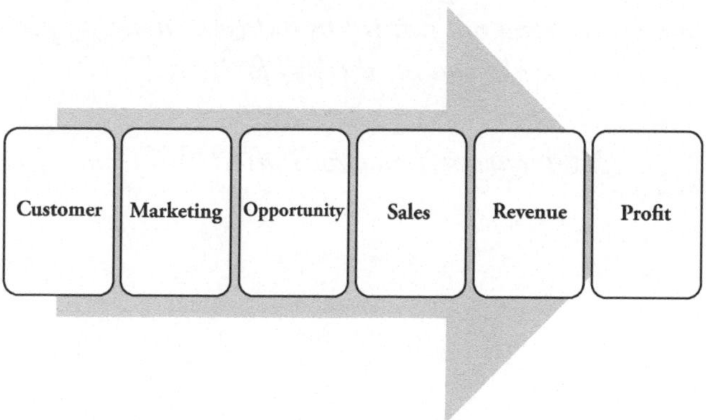

We can break opportunity into an acronym to explain the journey from customer to profit:

- Owner (You)
- Profit
- Perception
- Organization
- Relationship
- The Customer
- Utility
- Need
- Integrity
- Trust
- Yes

In the following chapters we will discover all these words, one at a time.

> *"Another piece of nuggets from author of G.O.L.F Mastering Business Success, AtulJee, a business design and growth coach, who not just trains but come down to pitch to make you hit the ball for a six."*
>
> **– Satya N. Gupta**
>
> *NGNguru, Chairman India IPV6 Council*

OWNER (YOU)

An owner is someone who discovers the opportunity and nurtures it. Some characteristics of the owner are:

- The buck stops with the owner
- As an owner, your ONLY job is to
  - See the Future
  - Create the Future
  - Build the Future

Let us have a closer look –

All functions of the business - Strategic, Executive, or Operational can be delegated, the direction in which the business must progress needs to be given by the top management who 'own' the business.

PROFIT

You may not hear it very often; profit is the reason for existence of a business. It is a financial gain; especially the difference between the amount earned and the amount spent in buying, operating, or producing something:

- Profit =Sale Price – Cost Price
- Profit is fundamental to a business
- This allows you to define where to draw a line
- Between the 2 Ps, Profit comes first, If No Profit, No Business
- Profit = PRO + FIT

Let us examine this closely –

The purpose of any business is to create value. Profit is a measure of the value created by the business. All sustainable businesses have healthy profit built- in. Some businesses do operate on a negative margin; there are strategic reasons for taking such actions. Some reasons could be – to create a new market, to enter a new market, to displace competition, to build a new ecosystem. There could be other reasons too; however this practice does not last for long.

PERCEPTION

Perception plays a crucial role in creating opportunities. Based on their perception, the customer may be willing to pay a premium or agree to wait for a delivery. Perception has a direct impact on the "pull" created in the market:

- A lot of effort goes into creating favourable perception in the market Brand Value - service, network, product, being on parity, value For money
- Sound delivery system-high availability of the product/ service
- Advertising/Social Media presence - builds good faith, communicates good infrastructure
- Positive attitude in customer-facing employees

Let us examine this closely –

It is always easier to build a business when there is a pull for the product/service in the market place. This in turn, happens when a lot of structured effort is put into creating this demand. For this, various engagements need to be examined in detail. Having a great perception takes many years of targeted and intensive work.

ORGANIZATION

An organization that is oriented to attract and create opportunities has following characteristics:

- Demarcation of work
- The founder/owner is involved in the design of the organization and does all of the planning
- The middle management balances between the planning and execution
- The feet on street take care of all the action on the field
- This kind of an organization ensures a balanced future

Let us examine this closely –

An organization that strikes a balance between the future and present is designed for growth.

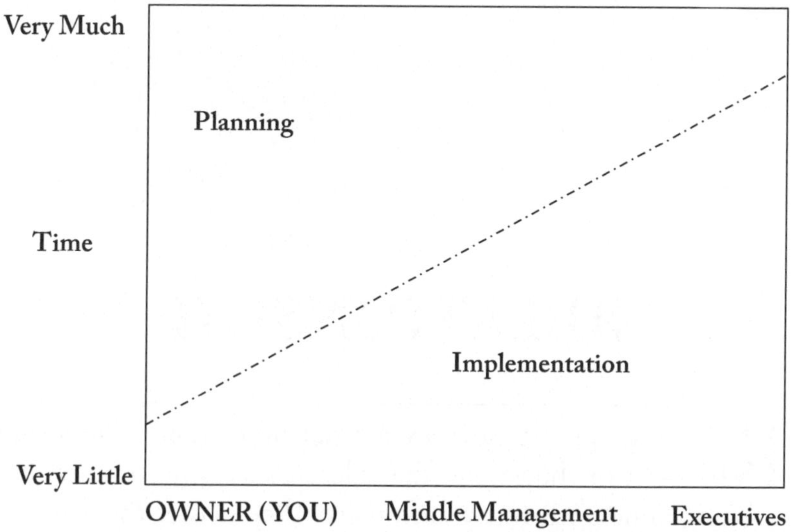

Atul Puri, The Author who master's his skills practical, smiles and laughs over his journey, where he walks but not alone, he gives opportunity building possibilities for not himself but for you too.

I am also a part of his learning as I have seen him becoming what he is Today, from dust to pebble, from pebble to stone and from stone to Rock and seeing him growing into a mountain top where everyone wants to reach.

Yes me too is the journey of you to yes.

Sure masters make the mark and Atul Puri is possibly giving us another OPPORTUNITY...☺

– Charu Gupta

Creator of CP Creations

RELATIONSHIP

Recurring opportunities are a result of a strong relationship between the buyer and the seller. A successful business has a strong bond with many customers. They master the game of converting a prospect to a partner. The early stage interactions are transactional. These build trust. As we deepen trust, a strong bond is established.

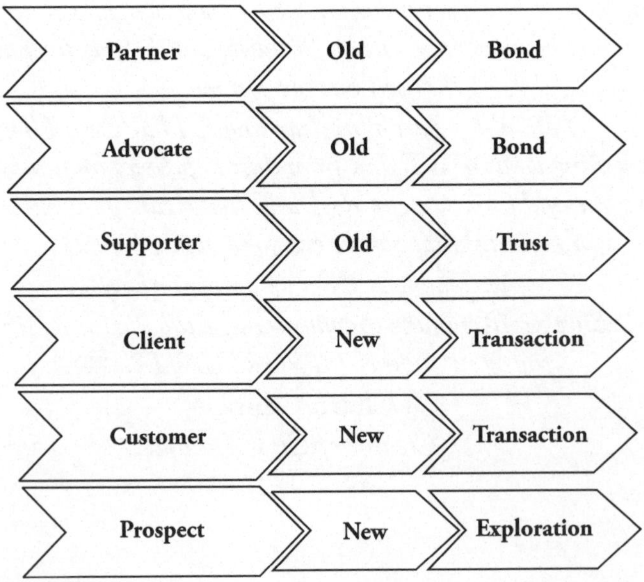

THE CUSTOMER

The customer is the reason for existence of the business. The customer is the only source of revenue for the business.

A customer is…

- The recipient of goods, service, product or an idea
- Obtained from a seller, vendor, or supplier
- Via a financial transaction or exchange for money or some other valuable consideration

A customer buys a product or service only if the following pre-requisites are met -

- NEED OR DESIRE to buy
- WILLINGNESS to buy
- ABILITY to buy

Let us dwell further on this -

As a business, we can service an existing need; may be we can expand it a little bit, some great businesses can even envisage latent needs and create needs.

The trick is to be in front of the customer when he is willing to buy.

As a business, we cannot do much about the purchasing ability of a customer; what we can do is:

- Make it exciting for the customer to buy.
- Make the experience awesome.
- Work on reducing the total cost of ownership (TCO).
- Total Cost is a combination of time spent, energy spent, money spent.

In today's world 3 letters which run the business are E.R.A.

- E – Experience has become very important. Offering a bad experience may be detrimental for the business.
- R – Relationships, with online and impersonal ways of conducting business increasing by the day, relationships have taken centre stage.
- A – Algorithms are here to stay. Those who grew up in the analogue era may find themselves misfits, yet the future is tech enabled.

UTILITY

A customer is willing to pay for a service or product only when the value is greater than the money the person gives in exchange.

- VALUE – How much something is worth compared with its price
- SERVICE – Doing something for customers but not producing goods
- QUALITY – A measure of goodness of a product or service
- CHOICE – Various options available so that the user can choose between them

Let us dig deeper

A customer evaluates the 'deal' in many ways. 4 of such parameters are: The value that they get on consumption. The experience that is derived from the quality of service. The quality, which is measured based on the finish, appeal, performance etc. And the customer also looks at what else is available and how much it costs.

The cost has 3 elements: Money spent, Time spent in obtaining it or configuring it and the Energy spent in getting it functional. So the benefits are measured against the total cost.

NEED

Need and want are very close to each other. While want is a desire, which is not urgent, need is something which is necessary for survival and can be fatal if not addressed.

- Necessary for existence
- Required for a safe, stable and healthy life
- A want is a desire, wish or aspiration.
- When needs or wants are backed by purchasing power, they have the potential to become economic demands.
- Nobody every died because of a want not being fulfilled
- In the case of a need, a deficiency causes a clear adverse outcome: a dysfunction or death.

Let us dig deeper –

A customer buys when they want to buy. As a business our job is to create an environment where the customer's needs are met. As this environment becomes more conducive, customers keep on coming.

There are five types of needs:

1. Stated needs: I want to have a Frappuccino Iced Latte - Tall (from Starbucks)

2. Unstated needs: Brand-consciousness
3. Real needs: I am low on energy, need to take in some sugar
4. Secret needs: To be seen as an upmarket consumer
5. Delight needs: An apple pie on the house

Passion in a subject is the starting point for any opportunity, be it Fitness, Photography, Problem solving. When one gets deeper into that subject, we realize that there are many opportunities to create a product or service, that can be a solution to many life problems.

Atul has done a deep study on how You can look for opportunities that can be nurtured and converted into a Business. Also, he can gone ahead to define how a culture can be built in your organisation that nurtures people to develop and grow.

I have read his previous book...GOLF - Mastering Business Success where he has focussed on how Business Complexities can be simplified, and make Life simple. His endeavour is to work, as a catalyst, with Business People in their Growth Path, where he understands Business Challenges.

This new book will have lots of strategies for various business challenges, right from nurturing stage to success. He is well-equipped to give the RIGHT Solutions.

– M.V. Narayan

Director NK Consultants

INTEGRITY

The state of being whole and undivided; Integrity is about having workability. For a business Integrity reflects like this-

1. State what you do
2. Do what you say
3. Do what is expected of you (may be unsaid)

Let us dig deeper–

Let us take the example of McDonald's; when we order for a burger, the system is set in motion. The bun is picked, the patty is heated, the fresh veggies are put, mayonnaise and sauce are applied, and cheese slice is also placed as per order. The burger is wrapped in butter paper and kept on the tray along with ketchup and some tissues.

McDonald's serves burgers and wraps across the world and this is all that they do. On top of it, they give tissues with every serving. This is what is expected of them. However it is not explicitly mentioned anywhere.

And the point to be noted is that the burger is the same across different outlets and at all times of the day. This is integrity.

TRUST

Trust is firm belief in the reliability, truth, or ability. For any business to run and succeed, trust is a fundamental element.

Stephen MR Covey in his book The Speed of Trust, says there are 2 dimensions of Trust – Character, and Competency

Character is the mental and moral qualities distinctive to an individual which hold him in good stead.

Competency is the ability to do something successfully or efficiently.

Let us dig deeper–

For trust to exist, both Character and Competency are required. Imagine the person/business is good- natured and is sound in character but there is a lot left to be desired when it comes to the quality of work (competency). You will not like to work with such a business.

On the other end if a business is good in ability but is low on character, even then it is difficult for the business to prosper.

YES

Yes is a sign of business being done! Once the customer is satisfied with the offering, they are clear that their requirements (needs) are met, then they consider saying a Yes.

As a seller I am focussed on what I sell, As a buyer the customer is concerned about what is being offered.

At any given time the customer is looking for answers to a few questions:

- What is s/he trying to sell?
- How much is it for?
- Why should I believe?
- What is in for me (WIIFM)

The moment these questions are answered for the customer and there is absolute clarity, the customer says YES.

Let us dig deeper –

What is being sold?

As the customers get absolute clarity on what is on the offer, they move to the next step;

What is the cost?

The customer looks at the total cost:

- The money the person has to pay
- The effort needed to get it functional
- The time it takes to get it up and running
- The opportunity cost

Is the seller trustworthy?

Once the product or service is clear and the cost is settled, the customer also looks at the trustworthiness.

The value I am getting!

The most critical factor is the customer's perspective on the value they are getting on the entire deal.

Opportunity – The journey from You To Yes is an unfolding process of our Perspective and approach for our Growth journey.

It gives us the Gears and wherewithal in not just identifying Opportunities but Leveraging the Resources for Cognitive Collaborative activities.

A great tool for MSME Business owners who are always challenged on Resources and time.

– Mr. Yogesh Udgire

Founder Digital Transformation Academy

WHAT NEXT

Wealth Creation

In the age of Leverage, Less is More. In this era 3 things that count are –

- Leverage – The glue of our business, it is all about creating more value for our consumers
- Opportunities – The buying environment to attract, convert and keep customers
- Wealth – The valuable outcome of leveraging the opportunities

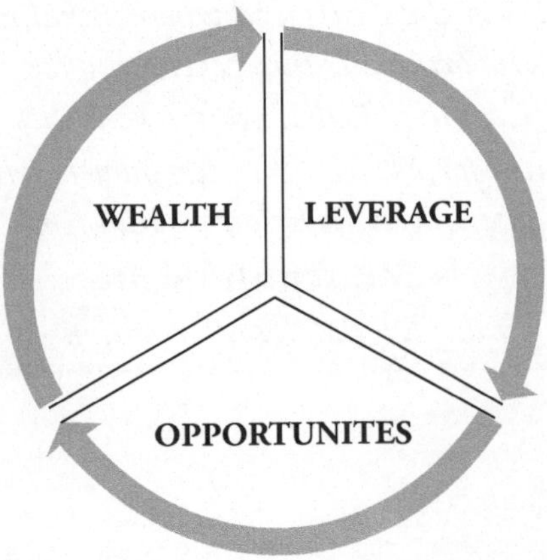

A subset of consumables used to create wealth is:

- Human Resources
- Time Investment
- Energy
- Money
- Infrastructure
- Material Resources
- Processes
- Intellectual Resources

To create a business for the future, you need a different approach.

Having worked with businesses form different industries and locations, I have tested The Leverage Model across a cross-section of Industries. This model is evolving into the art of designing the business for the future, from the future.

For those of you who wish to work further with the Leverage Model, I would be delighted to meet you over a chai and explore how I can contribute to your lifetime investment– your business.

Atul Puri

#548, Sector 56, Gurugram – 122011 India

+91 9899116054

atul@egrowth.org

ABOUT THE AUTHOR

Atul is an **Unconventional Entrepreneur** who believes, all businesses can experience exponential growth, provided they are designed well. He spends time building ***eGrowth – The Opportunity Network,*** a Sales & Marketing Ecosystem (SME) for Entrepreneurs. He also Heads Sales & Marketing at **MSM Unify,** an international education ecosystem. **MSM Unify** enables the stakeholders like students, higher education institutions and recruitment partners to collaborate online. Atul is also a Rotarian, as he is committed to open opportunities on this planet.

An Engineer, MBA of 25 years vintage, Atul has travelled extensively across the globe and driven **80,000 km by road,** across India to discover the pulse of MSMEs. This in-depth knowledge renders him an authority on how small businesses work.

Atul has evolved as a hands-on entrepreneur who has adapted to the rapidly changing marketplace - from Snail mail to Email to the 'Cloud' work culture. He is a small town boy, who had the fortune to work with the market leaders throughout his career.

He defines a CEO as one who consistently looks for COLLABORATION | EXCELLENCE | OPPORTUNITIES.

Some of the prestigious platforms where Atul has presented are:

Industry Bodies

CII, PHDCCI, FBA, MCCIA, MIA, PSAI

Startup Ecosystem

Startup India, TIE Delhi NCR, Startup Haryana, Startup Punjab, TSFE Jadugoda (JH), Startup Buddy Conference, CTR Ludhiana

NGO

Rotary Club of Mumbai Bravehearts

Talk Shows

Empowerment Talks Dubai, Midas Talks

Business Networking Platforms

eGrowth – The Opportunity Network, Entrepreneur Connect 2.0 Dubai, NBA Nashik

Corporate

Dalmia Bharat Group

Business Advisory

MSMEx.in

Opportunity – The Journey from You to Yes is a book about nurturing opportunities and the culture you build within your organization. It seeks to bring about the truth that only people who care about the organization they are in shall move forward in their own life too. The author has had experiences with many businesses and this is seen in the book. He himself has shown the power of networking in his life and the book. All companies and individuals who wish to make a mark shall surely benefit from this book.*

– Ms. Jamuna Rangachari

Author of 6 books, Software Professional and Journalist published in many magazines

REFERENCES

Here is a list of books the author has read along the journey. These books should be in the library of every entrepreneur. Some of these enable you to fly high; others inspire you to slow down before you take the next flight.

- What the CUSTOMER wants you to KNOW – Ram Charan
- The Game Changer – A.G. Lafley& Ram Charan
- Crushing It – Gary Vanyerchuk
- The Speed of Trust – Stephen M. Covey
- The Clarity First – Amit Chawla
- The Starbucks Experience: 5 Principles for Turning Ordinary Into Extraordinary – Joseph Michelli
- My Journey With Vada Pav – VenkateshIyer
- The Amazon Way: 14 Leadership Principles Behind the World's Most Disruptive Company – John Rossman
- Velocity: The Seven New Laws for a World Gone Digital – Ajaz Ahmed & Stefan Orlander

- How to Add 50000 Productive Hours To Your Life – Dr. Sanjay Kumar Agarwal
- 7 Habits of Highly Effective People – Stephen R. Covey
- Blue Ocean Strategy – W. Chan Kim & Renee Mauborgne
- Business Maharajas – Gita Piramal
- Fish Tales – Stephen C. Lundin
- Good to Great – Jim Collins
- Jonathan Livingston Seagull –Richard Bach
- Making Breakthrough Innovation Happen – Porus Munshi
- My Experiments with Truth – M. K. Gandhi
- The 5 AM Club – Robin Sharma
- The Art of The Start 2.0 –Guy Kawasaki
- The Five Dysfunctions of a Team – Patrick Lencioni
- The Lean Startup – Eric Ries
- The Professional – Subroto Bagchi
- The Road Less Travelled –M. Scott Peck, M.D.
- Who moved my cheese –Spencer Johnson, M.D.
- Zero to One – Peter Thiel